# The CIA

BY KIRSTEN W. LARSON

amicus
high interest

Amicus High Interest is an imprint of Amicus
P.O. Box 1329, Mankato, MN 56002
www.amicuspublishing.us

Library of Congress Cataloging-in-Publication Data
Larson, Kirsten W.
The CIA / by Kirsten W. Larson.
    pages cm – (Protecting our people)
Includes index.
Summary: "This photo-illustrated book describes the life of a
CIA officer, including their work recruiting agents and spies,
how they gather intelligence, and work to keep the United
States safe from terrorism. Describes real-life missions and
what it takes to get a job in the Central Intelligence Agency"
– Provided by publisher.
ISBN 978-1-60753-982-7 (library binding)
ISBN 978-1-68151-022-4 (ebook)
1.  United States. Central Intelligence Agency. 2.  Intelligence
officers—United States.  I. Title.
JK468.I6L37 2017
327.1273—dc23

                                          2015033078

Editor: Wendy Dieker
Series Designer: Kathleen Petelinsek
Book Designer: Heather Dreisbach
Photo Researcher: Derek Brown and Rebecca Bernin

Photo Credits: Zavg SG/iStock cover; Peter Jordan / Alamy
5; adwo / Shutterstock 6-7; AFP / Stringer / Getty 9; Jon
Arnold / JAI / Corbis 10; Sergi Reboredo / Alamy 13; PARK
JI-HWAN / Stringer / Getty 14; racom / Shutterstock 17;
jerryjoz / Shutterstock 18; Facundo Arrizabala / epa / Corbis
20-21; Monty Rakusen / Getty 22; Pete Souza / White House
/ Handout / CNP / Corbis 25; Stringer / Reuters / Newsroom
27; Dariildo / iStock 28

Printed in the United States of America.

The author thanks Doug Patteson, former CIA Clandestine
Services Officer.

10 9 8 7 6 5 4 3 2 1

# Table of Contents

# Getting the Bad Guys

Imad Mughniyah was a **terrorist**. He planned attacks that killed hundreds of people. He bombed the U.S. embassy in Lebanon. He blew up U.S. military bases in the Middle East. He even plotted the killing of a CIA officer.

For years, the CIA could not find him. Could he be stopped?

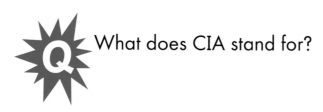 What does CIA stand for?

**Mughniyah planned the attack that destroyed this U.S. Marine base in Lebanon.**

 It stands for Central Intelligence Agency.

6

Yes. He could be found. Israeli spies found him. He lived in an apartment in Syria. The spies watched him. They told the CIA officers where he was.

The CIA had an idea. Officers would plant a bomb. The bomb would kill this bad guy. CIA workers built a bomb. They tested it 25 times. At last, it was ready.

**Spies found Mughniyah in the busy city of Damascus.**

The CIA officers snuck the bomb into Syria. They hid it in an SUV's spare tire. Officers waited. They watched Mughniyah. They tracked his every move. They wanted him to be alone when the bomb went off. That way no one else would get hurt.

After two months, it was time. Boom! The bomb blew out of the spare tire. This terrorist died.

Soldiers carry Mughniyah's coffin through the streets of Beirut.

**People eat at a café in Germany.
Is one of them a CIA officer?**

# Day in the Life

Many people think CIA officers have a cool life. They must drive fancy cars and fight bad guys, just like the spies in the movies do. But officers mostly try to blend in. If they work in other countries, they try to make friends with the people there. These people give the CIA secret information. It is called **intelligence**. This helps our government make decisions.

A CIA officer must be good at pretending. Only close family members know his real job. Others may think that he is a **diplomat**. An officer's pretend life is his cover story.

An officer can't talk about his missions. Even his family can't know. Secrecy keeps his sources safe. It keeps his family safe too.

 Does the CIA spy on me?

CIA officers don't tell their families about their missions. It's a top secret job.

 No. The CIA does not spy on U.S. citizens at home.

A tiny camera is hidden in a button. Spies can capture videos secretly.

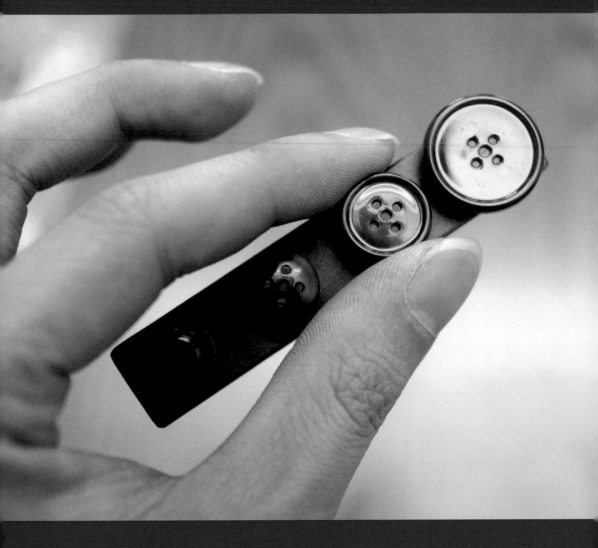

 **Q** Do officers carry guns?

The CIA uses all kinds of cool technology. Spies hide tiny microphones called **bugs** in pens, books, or flowerpots. Then they can hear conversations. They hide cameras too. They can snap pictures.

Today, cell phones make spying even easier. A spy nabs a person's cell phone. He swaps out the phone's battery. The new battery has the bug. Now he can hear everything.

Sometimes. They only carry guns in dangerous places.

# Learning the Ropes

The CIA only picks the best people to become officers. Only U.S. citizens can apply. To be hired, they must be between 26 and 35 years old. They must have a college degree. The CIA looks for people who can write and speak well. Finally, they must be able to learn foreign languages.

CIA recruiters check applications.
Only the best people get hired.

# CIA recruits practice shooting in all kinds of weather.

 **Q** Where do CIA recruits train?

New recruits train for at least 18 months. Some of their training is at The Farm. The Farm is a remote camp. There recruits undergo military-like training. They run obstacle courses. They shoot guns. They learn to drive like racecar drivers. They build bombs. Recruits jump from planes too. CIA officers must be ready for anything.

 At The Farm near Williamsburg, Virginia.

The CIA also teaches **tradecraft** at The Farm. Tradecraft is how to spy. Officers practice meeting **informants**. They learn how to get information from them. They practice making sure they are not followed. Then recruits may learn a foreign language. This could take up to two years. Then they can go **overseas**.

**The father and husband of these Russians was a spy. His death is mysterious. Was he murdered?**

21

**The CIA gathers information from many places.**

# Working with Others

Spying is just one part of the CIA's job. Other CIA workers study newspapers from other countries. They watch TV shows. They listen to the radio. They look at satellite pictures of other places. Then they piece all the information together in reports. CIA **analysts** study the reports. They try to figure out what is happening and why.

Every day, analysts give a report to the president. It is called the President's Daily Brief. The brief tells what could happen in a country in the future. It might warn the president about terrorist threats. Look out! Sometimes Congress asks the CIA for reports too. Many U.S. leaders need intelligence from the CIA.

How does the president get the Daily Brief?

**CIA Director Brennen (left) gives President Obama information his officers gathered.**

 He used to get it on paper. But now he reads it on his tablet.

Sometimes the CIA works with U.S. soldiers overseas. In the Middle East, a country called Syria is fighting a **civil war**. U.S. soldiers train fighters there. They teach the fighters how to shoot at tanks. They show them how to take down airplanes. CIA officers also talk to the fighters. They gather intelligence about the war.

The CIA helped train these Syrian soldiers. They also gathered information from them.

In the movies, spies might look like this. But a good CIA spy blends in.

# Protecting Our People

The CIA's job is to get information. Officers talk with people in other countries to learn secrets. Analysts gather information from spies and other sources. They tell our leaders what they learn. Our leaders use all this information to make decisions. The CIA's job is risky. But officers help keep us safe.

# Glossary

**analyst** A person who studies intelligence to find out what is going on and why.

**bug** A secret listening device.

**citizen** A person who has full rights in a country.

**civil war** A war between two groups of people in the same country.

**diplomat** An official representative of a government to a foreign country.

**informant** A person who gives secret information to law enforcement agencies.

**intelligence** Secret information about things going on.

**overseas** A country or place across an ocean.

**terrorist** A person who scares people with violence or threats.

**tradecraft** The art of spying.

# Read More

Goodman, Michael E. *The CIA and Other American Spies.* Spies Around the World. Mankato, Minn.: Creative Education, 2012.

McCollum, Sean. *The CIA: The Missions.* American Special Ops. Mankato, Minn.: Capstone Press, 2013.

Rudolph, Jessica. *CIA Paramilitary Operatives in Action.* Special Ops II. New York: Bearport Publishing, 2014.

# Websites

CIA Careers and Internships
*https://www.cia.gov/careers*

CIA Kids Zone
*https://www.cia.gov/kids-page*

CIA Spy Training
*http://work.chron.com/cia-spy-training-18536.html*

# Index

# About the Author

Kirsten W. Larson has written dozens of books and articles for young people. Or maybe that's just her cover story, and she's really a spy. Visit her website at www.kirsten-w-larson.com.